MILLIONS TO MEASURE

by David M. Schwartz
pictures by Steven Kellogg

HarperCollins*Publishers*

There are millions of things—
and many ways—to measure.
Let's fly back in time and see
how people measured many
years ago.

When prehistoric people held a race, they had to think about distance.

They wanted to know about size and weight.

Traders had questions about volume.

A bright idea was needed.

And so people used their feet to measure distance.

But measuring in feet could cause confusion . . .

because feet come in different sizes.

To measure weight, people used stones.

But stones come in different sizes.

How many seeds could a container hold? That's one way volume was measured. But some seeds are tiny and others are huge, so once again measurements could mean mix-ups.

841 . . . 842 . . . 843 . . . 844 . . .

200,001 . . . 200,002 . . . 200,003—there must be a better way.

Time for another bright idea!

Let's fly forward in time!

Kings, queens, sultans, sheiks, and chiefs solved the problem of measuring with feet of different sizes. From now on, they declared, only one foot would be used throughout the land.

Foot-length rulers were made.

Standards were also set for weight and volume.

But what happened when people from faraway lands worked together? It was hard to decide which ruler's ruler would rule!

Gradually people began to use the same ruler, no matter who their ruler happened to be. Now a foot was a foot whether you lived in Eastonesia or Westlovakia.

Here is the kind of ruler we in the U.S. use today.

The green snake is one foot in length.

To measure something smaller than a foot, use inches. A foot is divided into twelve inches.

The pencil is three inches long.

No matter how I stretch and squirm, I still remain a half-inch worm.

1/16

1/8

1/4

1/2

1   2

If you want to be very accurate, use fractions of an inch. You could measure to the half inch, quarter of an inch, and so on.